BREAK THE BIAS THAT BUCKLES YOU

Now, **Speak Up** Lady!

BREAK THE BIAS THAT BUCKLES YOU

Now, **Speak Up** Lady!

A CHRONICLE BY

DEEPIKA CHAWLA

Worldwide Publishing by

Pendown Press

PENDOWN PRESS
An ISO 9001 & ISO 14001 Certified Co.,
Regd. Office: 2525/193, 1st Floor, Onkar Nagar-A, Tri Nagar, Delhi-110035
Ph.: 09350849407, 09312235086
E-mail: info@pendownpress.com
Branch Office: 1A/2A, 20, Hari Sadan, Ansari Road, Daryaganj, New Delhi-110002
Ph.: 011-45794768
Website: PendownPress.com

First Edition: 2023
Price: ₹299/-
ISBN: 978-93-5554-444-5

Layout and Cover Designed by Pendown Graphics Team
Printed and Bound in India by Thomson Press India Ltd.
Creative Design and Illustrations by Amit Roy

PRAISES FOR THE BOOK

I have known Deepika for 18 years, and she has been an epitome of *compassion, action, and going above and beyond*, both in personal and professional life. Her energy, passion, and positive attitude is vivid and vibrant in this book as Deepika makes us examine that while the whole world continues to work around unconscious bias, unless women work on their own inhibitions and biases, nothing will change for them. I am sure the real-life experiences captured in the book will be very helpful for everyone in our society.

~Sanjay Khanna
CEO- Fortune 100 Company

***

Now, Speak Up Lady! is a beautiful compilation of stories that push our boundaries. Deepika beautifully threads together the issues women face in society, intersectionality of identity, and how our own internal biases impact the way we show up in the world. Each chapter offers readers a different perspective of every-day experiences, with D's Deal serving as a tool that encourages women to be the change they want to see...and taking ownership of their power. Very inspiring and thought-provoking read.

~Jiquanda Nelson
CEO - Diversity Window

Deepika combines personal anecdotes, hard data and compelling real incidents to cut through the layers of ambiguity and bias we surround ourselves with. Must read.

~Dr Ritesh Malik

Founder - Innov8

***

Deepika has a natural flair for helping women carve out a world of confidence and empowerment for themselves, thereby creating meaningful and progressive paths in their professional and personal lives. Deepika's work speaks volumes about her own experience that women draw inspiration from. Every reader, irrespective of gender will learn something that will stay with them.

~Vivek Pathak

Senior Leader in BPO Space - Fortune 100 Company

***

Deepika Chawla has transformed lives of thousands of people, especially women leaders, for the better. In *Now, Speak Up Lady!* Deepika has brilliantly captured principles of life through stories from her own experiences or what she encountered through interactions with others. These stories and D's Deal promise to offer to the readers a variety of perspectives, an opportunity to reflect, and an inspiration for them to take focused actions in pursuit of becoming a better version of themselves and the CEO of their lives. This book is the friendly hand that can help you live the life you truly aspire for.

~Arvind Agrawal

Business Leader & Mentor

Relatable to individuals of all genders, it is a page-turner that submerges you in the story and makes you want to unlearn and look at the world with fresh eyes. Well-written, and an easy read with immense depth, Deepika has been authentic and vulnerable, making this book an absolute keepsake!

~Gurnoor Kaur Behl

Creator - Online Personal Brands
Founder - House Of GKB,
Co-Founder - Delhi Queer Spaces

***

Her program 'Speak Up Lady', and this book is a testimonial to her tireless work and gives inspiration, shares practical learnings, tips and tricks that everyone can benefit from, whether they are aspiring professionals or just looking for motivation to become the leader they truly want to be.

~Philippa Mathewson

International Employee Engagement Expert,
Leadership Trainer, Facilitator and Coach

To my parents and parents-in-law for making me believe that I can fly, aspire, and work hard to make my dreams come true; to Abhinav and Drishti, from whom I learn every day and evolve as a better human being and a leader, and to my husband, Amit who has appreciated and respected the me in me.

CONTENTS

Out Of The Woods

D's Deals

ACKNOWLEDGEMENT

First and foremost, I would like to thank my parents and parents-in-law, who gave me the confidence and strength to dream boldly and live those dreams.

I want to thank Akshar Yadav, who said that everyone has a story to be told and must write a book not for others but for themselves.

Cathy Nicholls for always reminding me I can do it if I want to.

Amit Chawla and Amit Roy as my team for being great mentors and pushing me hard to complete this book.

Mary, Tasneem, Drishti, Lata Chawla, and many other mentees in my journey whose experiences and learnings have been shared here.

Sanjay Khanna and Arvind Agrawal for being a collaborator in driving Inclusion & Diversity and motivating me to grow in the journey.

All my mentors who have believed in me, held my hand, backed me, and pushed me into my discomfort zone so that I could prosper.

Dinesh Verma, CEO Pendown Press Publishing, and his team for their support and suggestions during the creative process.

And I am ever grateful to Sai Baba, who has instilled the passion in me for loving and living life to the fullest.

Break

AUTHOR'S NOTE

We all know being a woman is special. Being a daughter, sister, girlfriend, partner, daughter-in-law, a mother; every role is special. If all the attributes of a multi-faceted, multi-talented, ambidextrous living being ever trotted this planet, she must be a woman. If there has been a single repertoire of compassion, emotion, love, care, empathy, sacrifice, and suffering, she is none other than a woman.

Let's take a pause here.

These universal hashtags that have been infused into the conscious belief system of the society for ages seem to have played tricks in creating false alarms of sorts. The debate remains on whether it has resulted in keeping women tucked under the veil of excuses.

She somehow believes she's at the receiving end and has been denied her dues always. Does it mean that as a woman, she always needs to fight for her rights? Or is it merely a portrayal of haplessness, a sadistic reflection of self-pity? Is it surrender or sacrifice? No denying facts, is patriarchy a bad faith? If that be so, should rebellion be the only answer?

For a woman, is a relationship a compromise or empathy? Is it work-life balance or integration for her? With whom does the onus lie? What does #BreakTheBias conjure up to?

Unconscious bias: The whole world is working around it. But all said and done, if we fail to work on our own biases, nothing will work out. If we do not change, nothing changes.

Throughout my career of more than 30 years in the corporate sector, I have had the opportunity to learn, lead and re-learn from mentors, colleagues, and mentees, and all these above and more pointers have unfurled into a magic cube; each face showing up anecdotes of failures and success that propelled me to grow.

And every time, each phase has thrown up questions that forced me to ponder on the real meaning they hold. Unrestricting myself within the confines of my professional arena, I have had the opportunity to encounter life more closely, be it at my office, home or in my philanthropic endeavours. I found gaps that exist and torment, particularly women professionals, as they navigate through their hero's journey of struggle and success. Eventually, that prompted me to take the bold step of conceiving Speak Up Lady, a women's mentorship program.

Let me confess, it was a shaky start. I was both excited about the adventure and sceptical about the reactions. Will I be able to liberate the ghost called bias within my participants? Will they speak up? I was not quite certain. I waited for the answers with bated breath.

In the past year in the program, I have had the privilege to interact with more than a hundred women professionals. Representing various multinational corporations, primarily from the middle management cadre, surprisingly, these mentees have found themselves tangled in the aforesaid debate quite extensively. Mentoring them has been a whole new experience for me. While I listened to their stories, bizarre and dark, I was left with no other choice but to rediscover myself to motivate them to see the end of the tunnel. Introspection of who we are, why we are, and what we want as women needed to be carefully detailed.

Living in the woods and taking them out of it has uncorked life-changing episodes, moments, and memories. I could not let go of the opportunity to compile my journey of the Speak Up Lady program thus far and the stories that got churned out of it. A few are mine, and some have been shared by the participants themselves. That brings us to the purpose of my book, where I have drafted these stories with the participants' permission while plugging in my experiential journey as a woman, both in my personal and professional outfits.

So, what's the deal? Is this book just a compilation of events, or does every story call for a deeper introspection? Life is a journey of moments that shape up our life's narrative. We fall, we rise, we sustain, and then we learn that it's all about wisdom that eventually matters. Knowledge is just not education. Knowledge is clarity; clarity of thoughts, clarity to identify our true self. I have christened it as D's Deal. Simply put, it's Deepika's Deal to all my readers, followers, and mentees to unwrap the layers that each one of us nurtures deep inside us, relook at the mirror, and ask, who am I?

I earnestly hope that these stories will not just be motivating for every woman professional, but it's a way to deal with challenges, psychological or consequential, at home and work.

FOREWORD

I met Deepika many years ago as a vibrant go-getter in the corporate sphere, taking on and changing the world on her own terms. Over the years, she has evolved into a respected senior leader and, more importantly, into a mentor for women in the middle management rung to help them along their journey of growth and transformation.

Now, Speak Up Lady! is a compilation of Deepika's journey both as a professional and as a mentor, as well as some of the stories of her mentees. Having gone through the same challenges – that of feeling guilty of suffering from self-doubt, of having to balance the multiple roles a woman has to play as she navigates the work and home space, trying to succeed equally in both.

Deepika is able to take an empathetic and compassionate look at what happens beneath the surface in every woman's life. She presents a portrayal of the conscious and subconscious biases that exist in a woman's mind and in society, asking all to take a hard look at themselves while also recommending practical solutions to overcome these biases.

Research suggests that visible and vocal role models are amongst the most important influences for younger women to feel inspired and continue their journey towards independence and empowerment.

Each story in this book can claim to play this role and be just such an inspiration to foster self-belief amongst the readers. A gender which is more than half of the world's population and, despite that, is still struggling to fight their inner biases and become relevant, equal and meaningful requires all the allies it can get. This book is a significant step in that direction.

The stories of the demons that women face, both within and outside, the valiant battles, big and small, they fight; to live, to breathe, to make a mark for themselves, and even to reclaim agency over their lives and personal spaces will find resonance amongst all women today who are attempting to make significant strides in creating a more equal world for themselves and for the women who come after them.

~Apurva Purohit
Best-selling author and co-founder, Aazol

SELF DISCOVERY

And you? When will you begin that long journey into yourself?

~RUMI

ARE YOU
GAME?
?

-1-

SPEAK UP

Hit pay dirt

Idiom: To come upon something of significant value.

"If you tell a true story,
you can't be wrong".

~Jack Kerouac

You find real stories in real lives. This book is a compilation of stories from my real-life experiences and a couple of other generous fellow ladies who happily agreed to share their narrations.

As the book was nearing completion, the lay-outing was done, pagination got completed, and artworks were decided, I was discussing the marketing agenda with my team and Amit, but one thing was still amiss. All of us unanimously agreed to it. Even if I structured a prologue to set the context, we still needed a story to mark the beginning. Else, we thought, the journey would begin somewhere in between. A relevant story would mark a perfect beginning. But what would that be?

The inspiration lay in my purpose statement itself. What prompted me to come up with this book was the mentoring program I started one and a half years back. But the question was, what led me to conceive this program in the first place? What was the most significant episode(s) that had such a bearing on the overall agenda? I kept thinking and recollected every significant episode of my career since the early 90s.

In the film, *Journey 2: The Mysterious Island*, remember Gabato (played by Luis Guzman)? While on the island, in his bid to secure a small lump of gold that surfaced, he starts digging. But soon after, he landed up unearthing a gold rock so huge that he could never have imagined. No one can imagine either. As I reminisced, I started trotting the path of Gabato. **Speak Up Lady** is that small lump of gold that has surfaced as a purpose I nurtured in my 30 long years in the corporate world. What lies beneath is a profound bedrock that consolidated the program in its wholesomeness. It all started way back in the 90s when I was the only woman in the Bank branch office I worked.

It was somewhat a grunted feeling of loneliness thronged by a mélange of men. I initiated hiring temps, all girls, to mark my territory in the straight. As it unfurled, the team grew, more girls were hired, and I rose the ranks. But back then, concepts such as Diversity were quite in the embryonic stage in the corporate dossier, and I had little idea that I was mentoring them already on similar tangents. It was involuntary, and it came naturally to me.

As I transitioned in my career, my intent to mentor young women in their transitional journey became more pronounced. I took permission from my organization to get involved in more such activities, within as well as outside the corporate periphery. Diversity focussed organizations like BeyonDiversity and Lean In India approached me, and I happily contributed pro-bono.

The ripple effect was visible, palpable, and real. I was growing as a leader, mentor, and guide. Then the Ted Talk happened. It was June 2016.

I was invited to talk about the impact of technology and how it works together with the human mind, and how it will define the future. It was organized in one of Delhi's premier colleges, and I would be addressing a host of excited young students. I was nervous. Yet the preparation was in full swing.

'Speak Up even if your voice shakes'... I pinned up the poster on my desk as I locked myself up and strolled across my workstation. Back home, I was rehearsing desperately.

A day before my program, three girl students came up to put across the most unexpected request. As a group, they would love to learn how I became who I am. Tech integration was none of their concern. I reacted like, 'what?!'

All hell broke loose. The whole script had to be changed overnight. I struggled the whole day, and finally, I just jotted down pointers. I would build up on my story, I decided. That was the only excuse I could offer myself as a shortcut to win the day. But that presumed shortcut turned out to be the most significant turning point of my life.

On the D-day, my speech header changed to ***The Prevailing Presence of Passion,*** and it was my journey since I was 18. I narrated my roller-coaster ride, my dreams and despairs, my falls and rise, and my ethos and beliefs. I emphasized on three simple words, Resilience, Tenacity & Self-belief that drove me incessantly and helped me be who I am.

(YouTube: The Prevailing Presence of Passion | Deepika Chawla |)

By the end of my speech, I was overwhelmed with the responses; Ma'am, you no more seem a distant reality which we can't achieve... you made us feel everything is achievable...you're so real... etc.

I never realized I could make such an impact. I was both awed and caught in ecstasy. Egotism gave way to simplicity. Real-life stories could wield magic.

I wanted to continue the streak. As they say, the more you embrace the weird crazy things about you, the more you find your tribe... I never stopped, the tribe kept growing, and followers joined the caravan. So far, it was a happy run until the pandemic stopped every proceeding. The whole world gaped in distrust. So, did I.

Suddenly, the whole paradigm of personal branding, building relationships, everything I was so buoyed about, whatever I was gushing through as a mission, was challenged to the core. In fact, the very core was *not only shaken, but well stirred.*

It was an unknown world order which rejigged perceptions, lifestyles, and belief systems. Working women were caught at the crossroads of uncertainty, struggle, and frustration. It led to resignations, more and more with each passing and painful day. Whatever I stood for, whatever I promoted, everything seemed to wane way too soon. I realized that this was the time to stem the erosion. This was the moment to get them back to where they belonged. I couldn't simply wait and watch for the pandemic to be over and hope for things to settle.

What we needed was a focused and structured program to address the issues that were pivotal in disrupting the balance. I wondered, is it work-life balance, or should it be work-life integration that needs more emphasis?

Isn't it a life stage transition that had to be approached, decoded, and presented in a format that would not only help women professionals break their own biases but also would motivate them to speak up?

But the real challenge was to demystify the impasse; speak up to whom? To society, to the professional world or to one's own self? Let us not misinterpret speaking up as some sort of rebellion. Let us also admit that we as women have our own innate biases, which either hold the world as the culprit or we get sucked into self-pity. We need to focus on our own selves and learn, invent, and manufacture ways to deal with it. I felt the time was ripe.

This prompted me to design my mentoring program. This is it. This is what gave me my funnel of being alive and aloud. One and a half years into the journey of Speak Up Lady, I have over one hundred fascinating real-life stories to reshare and retell. And this, as we all agreed that day, my team, along with Amit, must be the story to start with.

D's Deal

For each one of us, our life lessons are markers of change; change of perspectives, realizations, and applications. But the extent we emphasize on the applications makes a world of difference. Is it restricted to our own selves, or do we go beyond and spread the word? Are we still in the garb of I, me and myself or do we feel the urge to evolve and check on the problems of a cohort in the society we live in? Problems do exist, but not every bit of it is manifested for obvious reasons and beyond. So, whatever we learn, we must plan to put up a success story and then, if you hear me, help create multiple such stories of triumph with people around. Are you game?

My Deal

PAUSE
CORE VALUES

-2-

IN SEARCH OF ME

Aspersion

Noun: An attack on someone's reputation or integrity.

The Imperial Hotel, New Delhi

July 2016

I was at the Imperial coffee shop. Everything about me, suited up in my professional gear, was near perfect. Taking a long, hard look into the coffee cup.... Cappuccino with hazelnut was one of my favourite combinations.... It was picture-perfect with the chocolate powder heart on top... The coffee cup did not have the typical smile. Because this was my second visit in a week, the hotel began to appear quite familiar, and my mind began to wander back to events from the previous week.

Previous Week

'Amit, an old acquaintance Reena, has reached out to me through my Facebook profile,' I exclaimed happily. 'She wants me to meet a film director. He is searching for a corporate profile for a lead role in his upcoming project. He looked at my Facebook page and thinks I'd be a good fit. I'm incredibly excited to meet him.'

'Really? You in a movie?! You should certainly talk and get specifics. Won't there be any screen test? That's how they go about the business, correct?' Amit remarked, sounding a sense of caution and doubt. I have been modelling pro bono for years to help promote diversity. But this was different, and Amit knew it.

I began dialling the phone while smiling and nodding to Amit.

'Now, who are you phoning,' Amit asked.

Later That Evening

Trrrring! My phone rang, and I raced to pick it up. It was the director himself on the other end. 'Hi Vishal sir, yeah, yes, we can meet tomorrow at 12 noon.... Delhi Imperial? Sure!'

'Yay, I'm meeting him tomorrow', I exclaimed.

Monday Afternoon

I walked into The Imperial Hotel on a Monday afternoon wearing my best business outfit, a little makeup, a smile on my face, and carrying my favourite Harrods bag.... With its white walls and resemblance to the magnificent ancient hotels of the East, this hotel always made me feel British.

The red-turbaned guard welcomed me as I strode enthusiastically into the coffee shop.

I noticed Vishal sitting on a table at the far end of the room with a view of the garden. I walked up with butterflies in my stomach but wore a confident smile. Corporate experience teaches this skill beautifully on how to remain poised in difficult situations as well.

Vishal stood up to greet me. After the pleasantries, I ordered my usual cappuccino with hazelnuts and a dusting of chocolate powder.

The introduction was completed, coffee was ordered, and Vishal briefly took me through his profile as a filmmaker.

I had already completed his verifications, authenticity checks, and reviews, as well as spoken with Reena about his films. I was at ease with the situation.

I questioned him about all of my concerns, such as how many days I'll need to take off, where I'll be shooting, and so on.

All of the responses pointed to an I AM POSSIBLE scenario.

The story session began.

'Look, Deepika, there's a stereotype that revolves around women in our society; either they are all-pervasive, or they are all passive. In either case, a woman is believed to be victimised. Whether you call that a bias or otherwise, the question remains a hot piping sizzler on every discussion table.'

Vishal paused and looked up at me.

'You are right. That's debatable'. I restricted my comment. I knew he was hinting at the most uncomfortable chapter, which is up for grabs at any forum.

'My story is not about the typical journey of a successful corporate woman but is punctuated by episodes in her life which challenge the status quo' Vishal was getting more intent with his delivery.

'And how's that?' I chipped in.

'Young confident woman, worked hard to complete studies with minimal resources, very intelligent and talented, rising up the ladder,' Vishal outlined.... 'gets married but....' Vishal paused.

'But?' I just picked up the bait.

'Apparently, her personal life seems balanced, but she's struggling to cope with her in-laws. That sounds commonplace, correct?' Vishal asked.

'Well.... honestly, it depends, you see....'. Before I could continue, Vishal took over. I felt snubbed but realised the discussion would swerve into a debate otherwise. I quieted down and allowed him to continue.

'While she's juggling between contrasts, I want to bring in the subtle innuendo, to be or not to be'.

'In one such conflict scenario, our lead character shares a few intimate moments with her male colleague during an official tour....'

That shook me up.

'Sorry', I said as I looked at Vishal.

'Well, the story demands that. The plot takes a turn, and that renders vitality to the character arc, you see.' Vishal quipped. 'Of course, that's not for real. A body double can be investigated if you are uncomfortable'.

My countenance, butterflies, and everything morphed into a large frown as I listened.

It was supposed to be a 60-minute film for film festivals, and Vishal had won honours and seemed excited with this screenplay. While the story progressed, I was still stuck at Sorry. It was an abyss least expected.

After 30 more minutes, Vishal wrapped up his narration and asked, 'So, what do you think about the end? In fact, I'm still unsure whether Aditi should quit. What's your judgement?'

I was not in the plot since then and didn't follow the journey.

'I will give it a thought', I managed the moment.

We exchanged a friendly handshake, and I exited the hotel, striding boldly, but now, with too much confusion in my thoughts.

Back Home

I arrived at my residence. I was quiet the entire evening as if I was about to enter my cocoon. 'How was the meeting? You didn't answer my phone, hope all is well', Amit asked as he hugged me.

That hug was probably all it took for me to explode, and I began discussing everything at the dinner table.

He listened as I told him everything. He stated, 'There are two sides to the coin, and you should make your own judgement'. He requested me to sit down with a piece of paper and write down my advantages and disadvantages... It's not that I didn't know I should do it, but there are times when you need someone to tell you what you're thinking. Amit got me to adopt this as a life-skill of journaling my doubts and clarity every time I seem to be at a crossroads.

I sat down after supper and wrote until 2 a.m. or beyond, and I had no idea when I slept.

Should I go ahead and do it or not? I remembered what Amit said, 'It's up to you, Deepika. I'm always there for you, we'll make it work either way, but you need to know what you want and who you are'.

The last two questions revolved around my advantages and disadvantages. Who am I, exactly? Is this a film about me? It prompted a new query. What is my most important value?

I was hesitant to put that message out there because, in my experience, it was not true in real life when it came to corporations. A lot of young girls looked up to me because they saw my life goals as their own journeys and destinations.

Why would I choose acting for a wrong message that I don't believe in, even if it's just a film? I don't believe we as women need to compromise or are just so weak to give in; we stand by our strengths, hard work, and skills, and we make amazing leaders and winners.

I let these thoughts linger for a few days until something struck my mind. Notwithstanding the fact that the story interrupts my belief system, is it only about my ethos? Is there a bigger picture I'm missing out on? Am I ready for such a change in my career? Will I be able to deal with the glitz and glam? If the film is nominated for an award, that's fantastic. What if it doesn't work out? Will that be too much for me to lose confidence as a leader? Will I be dragged into an uncharted universe full of uncertainty if the film's plot offers any hint? Will this have an impact on my personal life? Will my social beliefs alter because of this? Am I just scared, or is prudence making headway, finally?

I was no longer a newbie but a seasoned veteran. The detour was leading up to the prospect of making a hard decision, a career transition. In my mind, it grew to unassailable proportions. There was far too much on the line. I was neither ready for a picturisation which doesn't augur well with my outlook, nor was I prepared for a career transition which was dramatic yet intimidating. I am natural but can't act naturally.

That Weekend

I checked my watch. It was 9:30 a.m.

I began preparing to return to the Imperial Coffee Room to tell Vishal my decision.

D's Deal

Sacrifice the lure if it's beyond your belief. Challenge your own self, if need be, to discover the real you. That doesn't mean you necessarily sacrifice your aspiration, but ask yourself whether you would sprint up the tarmac of success or should you analyse the repercussions in advance; interpersonal, social, and professional. We tend to get blinded by the strobe lights of awesomeness. But I insist you pause. You may argue, what if I lose a golden opportunity if I let go of this? True, it's unnerving. Take a pause, think, consult, absorb, and then take your decision. If you are concerned about building your own brand, then it's just not you who makes it… it's the whole gang of followers who cheerlead you in your journey. So, it will be your clarion call to take it or let go.

My Deal

GIVE

-3-

BEYOND THY SELF

Break a leg

Idiom: A wish of good luck, especially in a performance.

New Delhi

February 2022

It was the Speak Up Lady and Clarity Meet-up, where we discussed the challenges and changes, we faced. It's an open forum where industry friends, clients, and mentees join the healthy debate and share their learnings. As my mentoring program completed a successful one-year run, I invited a couple of my mentees to join the tête-à-tête.

All the arrangements were neatly made for the 15 invitees. I was brimming with an overwhelming pride of accomplishment. The response my mentorship program garnered was immensely satisfying. It stitched yet another medallion of merit onto my successful career journey.

While I was busy shuffling between happiness, excitement, and a sense of pride, Tasneem wheeled in. She has been an acquaintance since Amit has been coaching her in her entrepreneurial journey for some time by then.

The semblance of vanity that was provoking me so far through the day seemed to evanesce the moment I saw her. My realization was spontaneous; here was one girl who remains the messenger of belief, hope, and empathy. She's a character born to script a different world order, much beyond I, me, and myself.

I still can't make out her secret of pulling out so much strength veiled underneath an unassuming demeanour. Her story doesn't seem anything less than a silver-screen blockbuster; a hero's journey of despair, self-belief, gusto, success and the never-ending urge to wheel on. With Tasneem's permission, I'm privileged to present her story as shared by her.

The Beginning

It was June 2015. Tasneem was employed with a multinational. That fateful evening she had an accident that changed her life forever. In the unintentionally obscured streetlights of Delhi, Tasneem lay on the road, bled, writhed, and then blacked out. She lay there, maybe for two hours or three, no one knows.

She doesn't recall who took her to the hospital. After a couple of days in a coma, luckily for her, she came out of it but was sucked in with a spinal cord injury. Her spine was damaged from T4 to T12, with L1 and L2 equally affected. Her bowel movement was disrupted, her bladder was non-functional, and blood and water collided in her lungs which had to be taken out.

With her ribs fractured, and her right leg suffering multiple fractures from the knee to the ankle, she had to undergo three surgeries.

If you hear her narrating her excruciating experience of those three months in the hospital bed, the stretch of depression she went through, you can but hold it up for a nightmare to hijack joy out of a 23-year-old.

Tasneem and her brother lost both their parents earlier, and the siblings were each other's sole support system. With life taking a wrong turn, their lives were thrown into the fire from the frying pan.

In addition to the physical trauma, she had to resort to a psychiatrist also to get bailed out of her precarious condition. That added to an overwhelming platter of daily doses that already had turned her taste bud pale. Her anatomy was jolted, and mentally she was down and out. Only a miracle could make her see the light of day.

Wheels of Change

Javed, Tasneem's brother, was the only hope she had. One day Javed wheeled her to the basketball court in the hospital premises. A team of boys, all in wheelchairs, were playing basketball. The sight was perplexing for Tasneem as she would look up to him for cues. Javed, being a sportsperson himself, probably had his hopes pinned on the court and the group of boys.

Javed would say nothing but let Tasneem watch those boys wheel past and basket. They would shout, celebrate, and enjoy their time on the court. Finally, Javed asked Tasneem to try out the sport.

Tasneem was quick to react in defence. She had never been into any kind of sports during school or her college days. On top of that, being in the wheelchair herself, with uncertainty lurking at every turn, joining those boys was unthinkable. She was scared she might fall. She had already endured enough in the last 3 months in the hospital. Given her condition, she was set for a longer stay there (which was one and a half years eventually).

Tasneem recalls that Javed has one mantra he owns and believes in: the worst-case scenario. When she rejected the offer, Javed explained to Tasneem the worst-case scenario if she agreed to play… she might fall and might have to undergo another surgery. She had already undergone so much. What else could be worse?

After a lot of cajoling, Tasneem finally agreed.

The basketball wheelchair is structurally slightly different to suit the sport. To begin with, Tasneem participated in a wheelchair race with the boys. But every time, she would land up losing. It called for a certain technique to bend and then propel the wheelchair during the race, and Tasneem could not bend as needed. That would drag her into further dejection. The trials continued for over a month until she finally managed to beat the boys. The sense of achievement propelled her to propel her wheelchair further, and she joined the boys in their basketball game itself.

Life had a different calling, and Tasneem decided to respond to it positively. The sport itself brought about changes in Tasneem both psychologically and physically. She could then move her toes and her lower body, below the chest, started responding to sensations.

In the sixth month, still in the hospital, her doctor suggested Tasneem participate in the 2nd National Wheelchair Basketball Championship to be held in Delhi that year. It was an opportunity that could open the floodgates.

Tasneem believes that every adversity has some opportunity, and one needs to grasp it while it's still breathing.

She took up the advice and went ahead into the championship. That was the first time Tasneem would participate in any contest under dazzling floodlights. It was exciting yet overwhelming.

Having practiced with the boys at the hospital, she had developed an edge in the sport by then. The journey into the contest was a dream run. She eventually emerged as the second-best in a well-fought tournament. Tasneem became the only wheelchair athlete in the country to have participated in the contest within

6 months of her accident. The Government of India honoured her with a medal and a cash prize.

The Next Big Leap

It was a moment of self-rediscovery. She could, by then, scale the steps of belief and live up to Javed's dreams.

Still in the hospital, the siblings started charting their next plan of action. They knew by then if Tasneem could do it, others could too. There are innumerable differently abled individuals across the country who might have resigned to their fates, putting brakes to aspirations whatsoever. The brother-sister duo formed their NGO by the name of the *Delhi State Wheelchair Basketball Association (DSWBA).* Their motto: reach out to those who are forced into a wheelchair and introduce them to this sport.

Tasneem knew wheelchair sport had the potential to not only unleash talents but also could break the bias one held. They organized an all-paid 15-day wheelchair basketball training camp in Delhi. Participants across the country joined in as they brought in their heart-wrenching stories of hopelessness, dejection, seclusion, and depression of years in confinement; at times for 10 long years in mental hell.

The outcome, as Tasneem says, was phenomenal. Post the training session, many of the participants went back to their hometowns to start their respective initiatives of wheelchair sports. Buoyed by the success, *DSWBA* has already organized two such events with international participants from neighbouring countries.

Besides sharing her story, Tasneem promotes the sport at various Government initiatives across India. Her initiative has been recognized and even shared over Twitter by our honourable PM in 2019. Tasneem has been recognized as the Wonder Woman by Vodafone Foundation, and she has also been an India representative, the first person from our country in a wheelchair, at the Global Victoria Women's Business Summit held in Victoria, Australia.

During the pandemic, Tasneem played the crucial role of liaising and arranging for all kinds of support for the differently abled, channelizing her contacts pan India and globally. Through her NGO, she's also actively helping people in wheelchairs get jobs with corporate and earn self-reliance.

Today Tasneem is hopeful of getting back on her feet soon. But till that day, she'll continue wheeling in the change discreetly yet bravely.

D's Deal

We talk about serving the larger WE, as in our community. But the moment the ME, as in our own self, is challenged, we recoil into our survival instincts. Only if we can bring out the Tasneem in us, we possibly may rewrite a script that can change pre-sets and mindsets.

My Deal

-4-

DIVYA'S IRONY

Hot-button issue

Idiom: An emotional and usually controversial issue or concern that triggers an immediate, intense reaction.

Hotel Corinthia, London

2018

I was on my annual vacation. With the temperature hovering around 23 degrees, July is always a good time to visit London.

The food court was laid out in the garden. It was located in the centre of the structure, in a large, curved courtyard that was festooned with fairy lights and green garlands that twinkle merrily in the evening. It was covered in enormous patio umbrellas, some of whose edges were almost touching. There was a marble fireplace with thick, yellow flames at one end. In this brave new outside world, it was, without a doubt, the best location.

We had invited Divya and her partner over for dinner that evening. I was meeting her after 3 long years since she had bid adieu to her parental home in Faridabad. Divya was associated with a multinational consultancy firm and was doing quite well. She was visibly happy and content. It was indeed satisfying to find the little girl grown up and settled. She and her partner, Vishal, were in a live-in for the last couple of years. Vishal was working in the same company as a Senior Associate.

As we binged, I was curious about their future and their plans thereafter. Notwithstanding the fact that we have supposedly progressed as a society, culturally, we still frown at disruptions and, at times, dwindle between acceptance and denial.

'When are you planning to tie the knot?' I asked.

'We are considering it soon, aunty… but' Divya paused.

'We will go for a simple ceremony… no big fat wedding.'

For a rich Marwari family (having strong cultural and uncompromising roots), Divya's intent challenged two critical aspects of the status quo; one, a live-in relationship, and two, a simple wedding without any showbiz.

Divya continued, 'Aunty, I do not want anyone pitying Vishal on the wedding day. Hence, I would rather keep it without the razmataz.'

My memories spiralled back to our neighbourhood in Faridabad. Divya developed vitiligo at an early age. It's a condition where skin develops white patches. As she grew up, life threw a rather difficult challenge. For a little kid, it was not only an embarrassment, but she had also been subjected to abject ridicule and bullying at school and everywhere she went. While little Divya silently sobbed it through, her mother, Rashmi, was fighting a battle of her own. Name any dermatologist across the country and she had visited them at least once. Every alternate medicinal route was explored. But Divya's disease was undaunted by any such intervention.

They were our neighbours. To me, she appeared just like any other kid in the locality; a beautiful, quiet little girl, full of life. But I never realized the trauma a taboo might ingrain in a mother's psyche. The very society we boast of the essence that the civic body accentuates as a philosophy, that cohort remains biased in its stance of truthfulness and acceptance.

Colourism is an ugly truth. They let her body hairs grow in the hope of hiding the obvious. Always attired only in longer sleeves and floor-length skirts, for Divya, sometimes the bystanders' looks developed into pity, and other times it manifested as contempt.

According to studies on the impact of vitiligo, 75% of persons affected consider their appearance to be somewhat to very unacceptable. Vitiligo affects a patient's appearance, negatively impacts their personal and social lives, and lowers their quality of life by causing social dysfunction. Their sickness reduces their sense of self and could make them feel ashamed in social situations.

Research Study reference: *This article was published in the following Dove Press Journal: Clinical, Cosmetic and Investigational Dermatology 2018:11 383-386 (Vitiligo and social acceptance)*

The report further substantiates that patients may experience emotional stress, particularly if vitiligo develops in visible areas of the body, like the face. Some feel embarrassed, shameful (with decreased self-confidence), depressed, or worried about how others will react. A study showed that more than half of the vitiligo patients declared that people stare at them, 20% said that they are labelled, and 25% said that their disease causes problems in their relationships with strangers.

At the same time, our society acts ruthlessly, with the least of prudence to precede judgment and verdict. When one of our common friends went ahead unwarranted and suggested her own interpretation of treatment, that too in public in broad daylight, I could barely believe the sudden glum on Rashmi's face. I could only sympathize. I felt helpless.

As a mother, we always remain biased towards our kids. We fancy an ideal state. That's natural. But Rashmi's state was unthinkable. We would not love to see ourselves at the mercy of society for no fault of ours. It's a nightmare, to say the least.

'It's how our society is, aunty', Divya continued. 'But here in London, no one seems to bother. That's such a nice feeling. Hence, we decided to get married here in London itself. Keep it simple. And that's it!'

Her comments left an indelible mark. It reminded me of body shaming. Is colourism an unfortunate cousin of racism?

Back in India, I pulled over to Rashmi's place one evening. I mentioned meeting Divya and Vishal.

'As a strict, traditional Marwari family, I am wowed by your disruptive outlook. How did you agree to Divya's live-in?' My question to Rashmi was rather point-blank.

'Deepika, I don't want anyone to marry her for money and leave her later. Let them understand each other well before formalizing commitment. My child has gone through enough. As a mother, I do not want her to suffer further trauma. That would be devastating', Rashmi continued.

'If London has given her that psychological space and individuality, given her an acceptance as a person irrespective of her disease, then I think that's the best that could happen to her. Her condition should not be a deal-breaker, despite what many strangers have warned.'

D's Deal

Colours don't define characters. Belief does.

In an ironic twist, in a culture enamoured with white skin, vitiligo is regarded as unclean, unsightly, and more of a nuisance than an ailment. Super models like Chantelle Brown-Young do lift our spirits, but only just like a plus-sized model would.

During my Speak Up Lady sessions, I have had participants with dark skins who were tormented beyond bet to even switch on their videos. Such has been their trauma. With Divya and Rashmi as my role models, I believe we do have a conversation starter.

My Deal

MIND YOUR LANGUAGE

Change your language,
and you change your thoughts.
~KARL ALBRECHT

Do's

Don'ts

-5-

THE GREAT GAFFE

Gaffe

Noun: A mistake that a person makes in a social or public situation, especially something very embarrassing.

For a generation like ours, Doordarshan was the only source of broadcast entertainment in the early 1990s. *Zabaan Sambhalke,* starring Pankaj Kapur and considered one of the pioneers of Indian television sitcoms, was a funny take on a distraught teacher who tried to teach Hindi to a class of students from all over India and the world. The sequel of eggcorn, malapropism and spoonerisms made it worth the wait every week.

We've often been snubbed or politely reminded to watch our language. Regardless, it has been our sincere intention to learn the corporate buzzwords in the process. We'd rather adjust to it.

Consider what happens if you're reminded to 'mind your language' (euphemistically) in the most unexpected setting and by someone you least anticipate.

The Pandemic impacted everything, forever changing how we established the world order. We didn't see it coming, though (No one did. Did you?). It would soon change yet another clear unconscious belief system I had. It all began with me being in my natural fluency.

Lunch @ Home

September 25, Friday, 1:30 p.m. 2020

I hurried to the lunch table after finishing my video call. Amit was already waiting for us. He would never, under any circumstances, fail to eat his meals on time. Friday's special cuisine was meticulously planned. All we had to do was take our time and enjoy our choices.

'I imagine your meeting went on for a while', Amit joked.

I reverted, 'Yeah... especially with this unique viral thingy, huh'.

'Drishti? Is she going to join us?' Amit interrogated.

'Drishti'... I called out. 'Dear, we're waiting.'

'She was working on her projects late at night', I explained.

'This is an extraordinary period. It is difficult for a final year student', Amit acknowledged.

Drishti lingered inside.

'What's new, Maa?' Drishti inquired as she picked up her favourite beverage.

'Huh. How did you figure that out?' Surprisingly, I inquired.

'Nothing. I only inquired'. Drishti appeared to be disoriented.

I had every intention of breaking the news in some way.

'Naved is coming to see us', I exclaimed.

'Do you recall that quiet boy from my CA days, Amit? He also attended our wedding'.

Through the cloud of his forgotten memories, Amit attempted to locate that friend of mine. But in his unsuccessful endeavour, he soon shook his head.

'And you know what?' I said softly, almost whispering. 'He's gay…'.

There was an eerie silence.

'Oh! Did I just nuke something?' I thought.

I cleared my throat and continued, 'He's now married and has a child. He's returning to Delhi after over a decade's absence'… It sounded like a cover-up to me.

'Are you serious, mom?' Drishti questioned, holding out her glass.

'Yeah....' I said innocently.

'I mean, when was the last time you said, meet Amit, my husband, and he's straight? Mom, when did sexual preferences become a topic of conversation or a part of introductions?' Drishti's eyes lit up in apparent disbelief.

'Yah…I meant that', I clearly fumbled.

The silence returned. It was a moment of paranoia that zipped my lips. Amit was quick to react and reset the context.

But I'd been nuked. I couldn't go on with the discussion any longer. I felt a wave of unease go over me. I finished the lunch in haste. After returning to my workstation, I pondered. It was a bit much for me to take in. The delectable menu's aftertaste faded far too quickly.

My years of patronising inclusivity and diversity, as well as my unwavering support for personal pride, all came crumbling down in a matter of milliseconds. My limbic brain, which has brazenly steered me in amplifying the obvious since then, had failed me the entire time in realising the truth: coexistence is inclusive.

I got into an unusual debate with myself. There isn't any pretension here. There can't be any. It's prudent that we adjust our viewpoints to reflect future sensibilities.

Fact file

- Was it simply a wrong choice of words or more visceral?
- Was it just the gaffe in correspondence language (with the new generation), or the outlook itself has undergone a tectonic shift?
- Is it time for reverse mentoring?

D's Deal

Mind your language. This phrase is to corporate verbiage and rules of expression always meant to delineate the unspoken limits of governance. In our personal lives, this phrase prompts frowns. Let me ask you, are we not biased by our innate beliefs of stereotypes and orthodoxy? Don't you think life has many more surprises than we expect? And when such disruptions shake us up, how do we react? Better be prepared, being flexible enough to adjust to the paradigm shifts. Else, be prepared for challenges you may never overcome. So, mind your language and work upon your thought process because changing overviews of gen next can become overwhelming.

My Deal

I can
I will
watch me

-6-

TAXONOMY MATTERS

Belt and suspenders

Idiom: Involving or employing multiple methods or procedures to achieve the desired result, especially out of caution or fear of failure.

Finally, We Met.

Nisha, Aditi and me, a perfect gang of girls, best buddies from school days, but sprinting in different tangents in style and thoughts right from the word go. It's a paradox how and why birds of (so) different feathers flock together at school (and then in college). Things change, and definitions of my type prevail and become pronounced with every passing day in our corporate and social life (later)... groups are created, relationships harboured, disbanded, and stories take dramatized detours that fox our fascinations of the past.

Yet, you tend to keep emotions at bay when you finally meet. The veil of refinement that after-life (till college, if we call it life) drugged us with may just lose ground for a few moments; giving way to chirpy chatterboxes.

But, with age, as youthful assumptions cement into tenets of life, contradictions erupt. For good reasons or bad, the whole belief system looks like an unworthy contraption of complicated engineering.

The debate must go on. So, we did — the gang of girls.

Nisha is a researcher in cognitive psychology and is based out of Hyderabad. She has always been a calm dove, intelligent and reticent. She was destined to pursue higher studies, and after a stint in Europe for twenty-odd years, she finally decided to head south. Married once, she never found it exciting, as she put it. So, she moved on.

Aditi, the bubbly beauty fresh out of the cascading waterfall, held her charm to date. What's your secret…just fits in perfectly as in a beauty cosmetic advert. Over the years, neither the TVC storyline changed, nor did Aditi. She's a socialite and is a facilitator of change, as she loves to establish. Her NGO initiatives cut across headlines and media forums.

The *ooh's* and *aah's* perfectly punctuated every interlude and pause as we gossiped. Emotions overlapped, giggles jumped the decibel meter… a couple of strange looks peeped in from different tables in the cafe, more bemused than otherwise… but that's all about us, the three girls from the city!

I was all ears but was preparing my script meanwhile. It felt like getting ready for the elocution test at school; here was one chance to secure the medal once again. An uncanny sense of competitiveness was poking me to go alive and aloud. The cafe turned into an imaginary stadium...abuzz with cheer as I was about to dart off; at least, that's what it felt like.

I started off in my natural, confident and (melo) dramatic fashion. Appreciate it. I had so many years to catch up and... I rattled off...how life changed course after college, my academic achievements, my stint in Switzerland, my struggles and stamina, kids, in-laws, husband...

'I'm lucky, you may say, but I worked hard towards it... now, my in-laws let me take charge of every situation... they trust my judgment, and it's reciprocating, you see... I'm thankful to Amit in every sense...he has never held me back... instead, he lets me be who I am, and they, Amit and my in-laws, all let me continue with my career...'.

Nisha interrupted in the most uncharacteristic manner (so much so I could recall her being in college). 'What do you mean by they let you do?'

I was baffled, briefly.

'What's wrong with that, Nisha? Yes, they do let me be!' I replied.

'That's the whole point, Deepika. Moment, you admit that you do what you like just because they let you do it, means what?'

'Means what? I don't get you', I was perplexed.

'Means you have somehow, subliminally, accepted someone else's superiority. Even though they are your family, it doesn't matter. Why can't you be confident enough to be who you are without someone letting you be?'

'You mean I become reckless and…' Nisha didn't allow me to complete.

'No! I never mean you to revolt. Putting up a stance is not challenging the other party. It's more intrinsic than you think. We have seen our mothers behave in particular ways. That has stayed with us. We have been taught certain ways to behave. That has become the unconditional and unchallenged beliefs we grew up with. We feel guilty of denial and are happy being conformists'.

'As a mother, you must be weighing heavily on your approvals when it comes to your children, correct? Dresses they may wear, things they may do, places they may visit, friends they may mingle with… you feel it's your duty to let them do things. On the contrary, you should refrain from being judgmental. Don't you feel hopelessly burdened by being a stickler? …think before you say it, believe before you do it…it's been quite long, Deepika. Do you still believe that you need others to let you be who you are? And what makes you believe that your kids are waiting for your approval to let them be who they want to be?… It's a bias. Grow out of it!'

I was zapped, and yet, at the same time, I could visualize my mini encounters with Drishti at home. Being a typical mother, when I would reinforce my flexibility of 'letting her' go wherever she wanted to or do whatever she felt correct, Drishti would pause and turn.

'Mom, if you think you let me do something, then you have not appreciated the real reason for me wanting to do such a thing'.

It would shake me up to the core, but even if we are being told, guided, and reminded of these refinements, how often do we remember to accept it and then apply it in our lives? Far too less, I guess.

D's Deal

What we believe in as parapets may not be valid from a broader perspective. It may not even stand a chance in future conversations and evolving societal matrices. What may sound simple, obvious, and rational may need a deeper introspection of root cause analysis, provided we can challenge ourselves to it. The question remains, will you let that be?

My Deal

-7-

DOWRY

Hissy fit

Idiom: An angry outburst; a temper tantrum.

Chapter 1

Let me confess when Amit and my in-laws came over to my parental home to finalize the marriage, I reacted. It was spontaneous. I had all plans for higher studies and no intent to get married.

For a determined girl in her early twenties, who wanted to lead an independent life as a girl, marriage would mean a lot of setbacks. At least, that's what I assumed. In fact, I was quite sure of myself. I let my emotions get the better of me. Honestly today, it makes me smile that even 30 years back, I could speak up.

However, Amit intervened. We went out on a drive, and I broke down in front of him. I poured my heart out. Amit has always been cool. He assured me he would ensure I could pursue my dreams.

To cut the context short, we would tie the knot eventually. But…

There was one thorn in the stack. And that blew the lid off me. My mother-in-law had a specific demand. Dowry?! I would exclaim in disbelief.

Yes. She was adamant. She wanted an iron chest for our new set-up.

Ridiculously silly! Why on earth would she be so hell-bent on an iron chest? I wondered. I was clueless but was never happy about the whole episode. With pent-up emotions, angst, and shrouded with curiosity and anticipation of the unknown, I turned a new leaf in my life.

Chapter 2

Nothing was familiar in my new house. Faces were new, the ambience was strange, society was an enigma, and freedom had a classic clash with a new set of norms. I was struggling to adjust every bit. I had my moments of despair. Had it not been for Amit, well…

I believe many of us have our unprejudiced share of credit for our partners, isn't it? Probably, that's the essence of a social union that humanity has designed to maintain balance.

Well, it seemed like a training institute where I would be introduced to a fresh new set of ideas and idioms, and I was supposed to pick it up without faltering. How insane was that? It was a tic tac toe, and I was either stuck or losing every game.

Chapter 3

Soon after, Amit and I shifted to a cosy two-room apartment at Saket. Finally, freedom was the call. A new independent life it was. A concoction of excitement, adventure, defining a new way of life, and experimentation.

One evening, while my mother-in-law was at our place, Amit and I were getting ready for a party invitation.

I picked up the dresses for both of us and was about to leave to get them ironed from the press-wala downstairs. My mother-in-law stopped me.

'Why can't you iron it yourself at home, Deepi?' She asked. 'You can save small amounts that way as well and be self-sufficient?'

I was a bit startled. Confusion and conflicting ideas ran amok in my mind. I couldn't make out whether to conclude it as guidance or order... whether she was rude or wise?

'But we do not have an iron board Mumma, I replied after a pause. It was a genuine excuse (oxymoron, it may sound).

Then came the surprise of my life. Mumma asked me to take out the trunk she asked for (dowry). She neatly covered it up with a folded bed sheet and asked me to plug the iron. The press stand was ready in no time.

I was so impressed by how she simply converted the trunk into a beautiful table which could be used for pressing. I have been tempted to share this seemingly insignificant story, primary to uncover those dusted episodes locked deep inside our closets of life. You must have similar experiences. Do you remember any?

We are too quick to jump to conclusions which may be blinded by our own delusions, isn't it? How many such so-called insignificant episodes do you recollect? How many times have you felt bad because your judgment about someone turned out to be incorrect to the core?

The Swiss Beckoning

Within six months into our marriage, Amit was assigned to a project in Switzerland for a year. Now, that meant something. While freedom was the clarion call, just two of us in an unknown terrain was a subtle dampener.

We took off for the Alps.

The breath-taking beauty, the ski wonderland, the decadent chocolates, and the land of watches are just a repertoire of amazement to watch out for.

After the initial euphoria got over, I settled down. The moment I opened the windows, an unfamiliar chill would greet me, reminding me of a not-so-cosy reality.

Amit went off to the office every morning. So do all of us (sic). Being a good-wife, I was supposed to get his clothes ready every day. You may wonder, what's the big deal, Deepika?

Now that's where the table turned on me! Being a newly married girl, in less than a year, I was stranded amidst a pile of clothes and a hoard of helplessness. On top of it, I had to save as much as I could. So, taking the liberty of a laundry shop was a way too luxurious deal in possibly the most expensive country. I recalled that episode of the iron chest-cum-iron board back in Delhi. I quickly turned the table on, and my iron stand was ready.

D's Deal

We are often biased by our own interpretations, presumptions, and premonitions. We become judgmental of people and situations. As women we are groomed to be conservative with our perception, which may be limited by knowledge and experience. However, time reveals the truth. At times, it hits hard, and later, it heals. It's valid in both the personal and professional spaces we operate. It's prudent not to jump to conclusions fast. You never know, events may surprise you.

My Deal

GRIT

The question isn't who's going to let me;
it's who's going to stop me.

~AYN RAND

NOT GOOD ENOUGH
WHY ME?
LOW ESTEEM

-8-

LOVE. LABOUR. NOT ALL IS LOST.

Foot in the door

Idiom: To find an opportunity to make progress in a desired direction.

New Delhi

January 2022

A sunny morning would just be the perfect setting in Delhi winters. The pandemic still cast its shadow of uncertainty and couched us up indoors. It's punishment! But who dared risk the laws?

The sun was gentle, and the chill was relaxing. It is a mixed realism that teleports you to a world full of colourful chaos… and there you sit down to rearrange every element and create a movie reel… then you sit back and appreciate the masterpiece as an audience, cheer yourself as a director, and reward yourself with the golden lady in front of a larger audience… you dream with eyes wide open.

Wish life would have been so much a fantasy… wish there would be a magic wand to sprinkle the glittering stars and awash it with all that's impossible!

I was waiting for Laxmi to join my online mentorship session. She enrolled a couple of months back.

Laxmi shared her reel in our very first conversation. The start of her show reel was simple and unassuming, and one could easily tag it as average. But you are never allowed to peep into the secret closet called life. Imagine yourself standing in the central lobby of a multi-storeyed locker room. Rows of closed vaults pan out relentlessly and vanish beyond what your eyes can fathom. That's your library of life. You have the keys but are allowed to open each of these vaults only in sequence. Can you imagine that scene?

Laxmi's Vault

That's how Laxmi's vaults of life unfolded.

After faring well in her schools, she enrolled for CA. Although she aspired to become either a scientist or a pilot, she was neither privy to nor had any mentor to guide her properly to pursue her dreams. Moreover, she dreaded Physics as a subject. Her father being an accountant, suggested she take up Commerce and subsequently pursue CA.

She cleared the foundation and the subsequent levels and bagged a good Articleship. Somehow, she slacked a bit in clearing the finals, though. Finally, she graduated as a professional CA in 2007. Her entire family was elated at her success. She was the first person to do so from her family.

She appeared for a couple of job interviews and finally got selected by one of the private companies on the last day of campus hirings. With another hurdle cleared, she got rolling with her career in the shared services industry. In her stint with two companies, she not only learnt the tricks and matrices of the trade, but she also got the opportunity to travel abroad as a part of her assignments.

Even though she had an exciting journey, it sounded all so average.

Laxmi continued, 'Around 2010, while I was associated with the second organization, there was a sudden restructuring in the organizational structure. IIM graduates, along with professionals from the Big 4 companies, were hired and inducted into the current team. This resulted in the redundancy of existing roles. I was told to venture out for opportunities outside the organization', Laxmi paused.

'I was not prepared for this sudden setback. I took leave and started knocking on recruiters across Delhi. At times, days were idle as I would wait for that one illusive call from a recruiter'.

'My confidence stumbled as the days rolled by. I was sinking into depression and started doubting my credibility. Negativity was choking me every moment. My notice period in my last organization ended, and I was still jobless. Five months passed by. My friends, however, were my ultimate support and one day, I got an interview call from a renowned BPO through one of my friend's references. The interview went well. I was to relocate to Bengaluru'.

'Meanwhile, before this career jerk, life inducted another fresh start. I got married. 3 years went by, and my differences with my partner grew deep. He wanted to relocate to the US, while I, being the shy girl I always had been, never wanted to give up on Delhi and India. Finally, we separated'.

'So, when this opportunity in Bengaluru surfaced, I thought to give myself the push to break my psychological inertia. My parents always encouraged me to move out and explore, but I never dared. By then, it was the best time to go out and explore. So, I did'.

'It was tough to leave the city I grew up in, leaving behind the friends who were an inseparable part of my life, the food, and the noise. However, Bengaluru was exciting, particularly the weather and the people around. I checked in at the office hotel and soaked in the vibes of the city. I let go of the bad memories of a broken marriage and job loss. It was a new start'.

'It was a new work environment and a new cultural set-up, and coupled with global exposure, I soon settled in comfortably. Things were smooth. There was a work-life balance. My parents also liked the city before I invited them to stay with me at my newly purchased apartment'.

'Thus, the shy, timid girl with low confidence had grown up to take on the world. I was managing several things independently and was helping people in whichever way I could. I was amazed at my own growth as I got actively involved in my housing society's cultural activities and became a popular girl who was an inspiration to many'.

Losing Out, Yet Again

All of a sudden, the world came to a halt. The pandemic pulled its break on everything mobile, sensible, and normal. The project on which Laxmi was working had ended as the client had gone bankrupt. She was temporarily assigned to another project with the hope of getting something new soon.

'One Friday evening', Laxmi continued, 'I received an invitation from my manager for a call with HR on Monday. I spent the whole weekend worrying and preparing myself for the call. I had listed down all my achievements assuming that it might be a performance review call. I was worried, nonetheless'.

'It was Monday, 17th August 2020, at 10 a.m. The call started. My manager nonchalantly said, 'your role has become redundant, and we don't have any more projects to offer. Please submit your resignation. We will offer you a severance package'.

'The entire world seemed to collapse around me. After investing endless hours, going those extra miles, and putting all my energy into it, I was being asked to leave because the company did not value its most valuable asset!' Laxmi gasped for breath.

'So, just one fine day, my credentials vanished. I was asked to surrender my laptop in the office. No one in the team was aware of this. I kept getting calls and messages from colleagues enquiring about my whereabouts. I was not in a state of mind to talk to anyone. I later came to know that several others too were asked to leave in a hushed up manner by the company'.

Back on the Terrace

Hi Deepika… Laxmi's voice on the screen suddenly got me back to the present. She smiled on camera 'Guess what? I have found a job, and I am joining tomorrow'.

A gleaming Laxmi continued, 'Deepika, you told me to record my session, and as I heard and reheard my story, I realized I had done so much and always came out head held high in every situation… Then, why am I nervous? Why am I questioning my worth? Just because a company had asked me to quit. How can they value me, or anyone else for that matter, if I don't value myself? I have been networking and meeting new people, and here I am'.

I don't know where life will take me here-on, but one thing is certain that I will not let anybody undermine me in any way. If a job doesn't suit me, I will explore opportunities elsewhere. If I don't get along with someone, I will look out for better partnership… In short, I will stay firm, stay positive.

Laxmi went on for 30 minutes, but I was enjoying it as a dramatic show reel on the silver screen unfolding through a roller-coaster.

D's Deal

Laxmi was the 4th mentee who had undergone similar stress post losing her job during the pandemic. It forced them into self-doubt as the obvious worries that shrouded them were:

- Why Me?
- Am I not good enough?
- Was I bad at my work?
- I have lost my confidence
- It was probably due to my skill set
- Will I ever get a job?
- My life is done for
- There is something wrong with me

But remember these: Losing a job is deeply shocking. It is a loss of livelihood: the ability to support ourselves and often our families. But the emotional impact goes beyond financial stress. For many of us, work offers valued meanings and relationships and when work suffers a jolt, so do all these associated emotions, prompting us to fret as well as leave us deeply saddened at leaving people, projects, and a place to which we have given a large part of ourselves. But perhaps the most significant is the impact of job loss on our identity or sense of self. For many, work is not only a large part of our waking hours but also who we feel we are.

This is especially true if we were engaged in a job we loved or where we built a career over the years. The loss of this identity can be devastating.

When in such a crisis, just remind yourself:

- When we go through life stage transitions, like losing a job, we can pause and think of something similar or any impossible situation we may have experienced earlier. How did we tackle it back then?
- We try to live in denial. Acceptance of what is happening is a big step.
- The journey to move from denial to acceptance, to commit to act on ourselves, will help us be stronger.
- We all have similar backstories in our lives, but we always forget them when a sudden change occurs.
- There is a lot more happening worldwide and in organizations across, and there could be multiple reasons why we are reengineered. The reasons are beyond us.
- Work on your networking and actively work on your LinkedIn profile.
- And finally, I asked Laxmi to record her storytelling session with me and listen to her own life story over and over again. That worked for her. It will work for you too.
- Find a mentor who can navigate you through such tough times.

My Deal

-9-

MARY

If worse comes to worst

Idiom: If the worst possibility should occur

Home

2013

The next day was Abhinav's IIT entrance exam.

At around 4:30 p.m. Mary, our house-help for fourteen years then, started vomiting and soon fainted outside the kitchen. It was a sudden panic situation. The next day was critical, and as parents, we too were nervous about the exams.

Wisdom prevailed, and I didn't want to take any risks. We immediately took Mary to the doctor in our neighbourhood. Post diagnosis, the doctor looked at me and said that Mary had a heart condition and she needed to be hospitalised immediately.

I was clueless as the doctor didn't elaborate much on her ailment. I jumped back into the car along with Mary and called up Amit to inform him that I was taking her to the Metro Hospital at Faridabad.

Mary was rushed to the emergency as soon as we reached the hospital. I came to know of a disease known as the rheumatic heart, which Mary was suffering from. The doctor explained that if a child suffers from rheumatic fever at the age of five, under certain circumstances, the heart valves stop functioning when one reaches forty; in the case of Mary, 3 valves in her heart needed to be replaced.

If that simple piece of medical terminology wasn't enough to drive me crazy, the doctor further said that Mary would not survive the night. Amit and I tried to reach out to Mary's family back in her village in Jharkhand. No one could be contacted. After a prolonged attempt, her husband responded but could not make it till the next day.

It may sound frustrating to even anticipate such careless behaviour from her family, but the social dynamics of certain strata of our country are quite complex.

While Mary struggled in the ICU, I spent the night sitting on the stairs, praying for a miracle. Amit was shuffling between the hospital and home, attending to Abhinav, trying and calming things down. The next day was Abhinav's entrance exam.

The Next Day

Mary survived the night. But the doctors were reluctant to carry out the surgery. It was way too critical, and the chances of her survival were sparse.

Amit stayed back at the hospital while I was frantically calling up possibly every connect. We had to find a solution; a hospital which would agree to operate on her. It was a valve replacement procedure, and not only was it critical, but expensive too.

Lying on the bed, Mary would just say, 'Didi, I want to live'. Tears kissed her cheeks, and I would hold her hand in silent but gritty support.

I was ready to spend any amount on Mary. She had been a part of our family, a mother to my children. While I was away spending long hours at the office, Mary would take care of everything back home. I would not let it go so easily.

But the hospital refused to operate. We had to take Mary back home after three days. She wasn't well.

We were trying to figure out a hospital which would agree to this critical surgery. We approached the Rotary. But nothing worked out as no one would agree to own up to the major surgery.

As desperation ticked on and all possible options dried up, I felt that the only place could be AIIMS. But I knew no one there whom I could approach. Given the severity of Mary's condition, each day was worth a billion.

The Last Hope

That was the first time I ever visited India's premier medical institute. The rules were the same for everyone. I had no privilege, either.

I got Mary to wait in the car as I stood in the queue. I could not manage a coupon on the first day. I later learnt that I had to wait in the queue from 5:30 in the morning, get a coupon, and the doctor would see patients from 11:30 a.m. onwards.

Finally, we managed to consult a heart specialist. They put Mary on blood supply. But that wasn't enough. We needed a surgeon who could operate on her. I was unable to get through to the right connect. I dialled up my friends for references. I talked to anyone I could get hold of there to try and find out a surgeon.

Three days passed. Every day I would wait in the ground, eat from the canteen. Hours rolled by, and I was losing Mary.

One day a young Sikh doctor came up to me and said, 'I have been observing you for the past couple of days. And I can see your patient is on blood transmission. You don't look like family…so what's the story?'

I told him about Mary and the entire backstory. He took Mary's file from me, checked it and guided me to a room where there was NGO support available for the underprivileged. They asked for a few documents of Mary to validate her status. I tried to get those from her native place, but they could not help. In desperation, I had to call up my friends in the Government department, who eventually helped arrange the necessary documents.

Once the paperwork was done, I had to seek help of my friends again in the medical fraternity to fix an appointment with a heart surgeon.

After a traumatic week-long endeavour, Mary finally got operated on, her valves were replaced, and she was discharged from AIIMS after 7 days.

Besides the initial investment, AIIMS took care of her complete medical expense, right from the surgery to her treatment, till date. Mary survived.

She's still with us for 23 years now. She remains a part of our family. We sent her back to her village once, but she returned soon. She loves staying with us. AIIMS is her only place to get treated.

D's Deal

Remember the famous movie dialogue, *'Kehte hain ki…agar kisi cheez ko dil se chaaho toh puri kayanaat usey tumse milane ki koshish mein lag jaati hai.'* (it's said that if you wish for anything wholeheartedly, then the whole universe comes to help).

Mary wanted to live. We all wanted her to live. The grit, the resilience, and the struggle bore the results of a life being saved. It was all about a woman who loved her life so much. A soul who was determined to survive the night and see the daylight.

When we decided not to let go despite the improbable, the whole community came up to our rescue. My friends, my family, and the Government department at Faridabad that helped get Mary's documents done for the NGO. The NGO ensured Mary got the benefits that were her due. The doctors helped her survive. And how can I forget that Sikh doctor who guided me to the NGO when I had lost all hope?

It's the belief that won us the day. It's the belief that will surely help you win your day too. It's the love for a human being, unbiased by her status or religion, that will help salvage the most precious relation we so often ignore. Mary was (and remains) our inspiration of grit and indomitable spirit to challenge the inevitable. You may say it's her destiny that she survived. But it could be she challenged her destiny itself.

My Deal

You Can Do It!

-10-

THE MAGIC MOMENT

Go the whole hog

Idiom: To do something as completely as possible.

Around 10 years ago

IIM Lucknow

Whenever I say that one must work hard towards anything they want, Amit counters by saying that *'Galat mehnat nahi karni chahiye.* You should not break the rules to be somewhere'.

This is in context to one incident that had a profound impact on me, and it will stay with me forever. It not only empowered me as an individual, but it did also infuse a lot of self-belief as a leader.

Getting to IIM

As a young kid, it was my dream to pursue MBA. Life took turns, and I graduated as a CA instead. But old habits die hard. So do cherished dreams. The opportunity finally came when I was selected to be part of a 5-day Strategic Leadership Crash course at IIM Lucknow, on behalf of my organization. The deluge of satisfaction was overwhelming, to say the least.

I landed up at the expansive campus, and the student's room was equally cosy to add to my wonderment. Have you not felt overwhelmingly satisfied when you get an opportunity to be back at the campus long after you bid it goodbye? That sensation of reliving the good old young self is so satisfying, isn't it? Precisely! That's what made it a fulfilling agenda. But I had no clue what was waiting to surprise me. And at the end of it, it was not only those incredible 5 days at the campus and the knowledge I absorbed, but it was one moment that mattered so much.

The Preparation

The day I landed at the campus; I could see a lot of security preparedness was under way. The campus was under strict vigilance, and there were busy feet and sharp eyes scanning every corner. It was quite intriguing.

Curious as I always have been, I went up to the security guards to enquire about the reason for such busyness.

'Tomorrow, Dr. APJ Abdul Kalam sir will visit us and address the students', came the reply.

My jaws dropped in disbelief. For a fraction of a second, I was lost in my thoughts of the aura that Kalam sir exuded whenever I saw him on TV or YouTube.

I regained my senses (sic) and rushed to the admin office.

'Can I meet Kalam sir tomorrow?' I asked politely.

'Sorry, you can't. Only students are allowed, and seats are full', came a point-blank reply. 'But I too am a student here for 5 days', I fought back with my logic.

The ice would not melt. I could not convince them with all my arguments. Rules were rules.

I returned to my hostel room with a kind of heavy heart. It was, possibly, for the very first time, I was denied what I desired. Ask for it, that's what I keep reassuring my mentees. Till the time you ask for anything you desire, no one's going to facilitate it for you. But that day, I was rejected.

D-Day Morning

I accompanied one of my colleagues and a co-student for a morning stroll on the lush green campus lawn. The morning dank made me tuck into my pullover. The city noise struggled to pierce through the serenity of the campus, reinstating the prerequisite of a seat of knowledge; unpolluted, undisturbed, calm.

The security was beefed up. The pathway laid in perfect harmony in anticipation of the honourable guest. It was the highest protocol that the former state head was honoured with.

All of a sudden, the action seemed to pick up the pace. Security was in position. I could see the gentleman get down from the vehicle. He was immediately accompanied by a convoy of Z-security personnel as he started his walk down the pathway.

Butterflies, cramps, horses, you name, any concoction of emotion possible, all started forming and fuming within me. **He didn't carry the aura of a film star, but he had the Wings of Fire, he Ignited Minds, and he was the true proponent of the Indomitable Spirit.**

I watched Dr. Kalam from a distance as he walked down in his customary brisk steps. I knew I could only see him and miss the opportunity of meeting him in person unless...

'Go for it, was the inner calling.'

It would mean breaking the rules and demeaning the protocols. It would be a crime. But I couldn't hold myself back.

I'm five feet. So I could duck easily. I was unusually swift at that very moment. I dodged the security, and I ran until I stopped just in front of the great man. The security, administration, and other students were witness to this most unprecedented act (of audacity) in disbelief. Two sturdy security personnel were running at me.

Dr. Kalam gestured at them to push back.

After the pleasantries, Dr. Kalam shared a piece of advice; 'People like you who have the desire to outdo must give back to society in whatever way you can'.

What a moment! What a man! What a legend! An incredible piece of advice! It got imprinted in my psyche.

D's Deal

It is about challenging yourself, not protocols. That will be a crime. But when your desire for something great overpowers you, go for it. Remember, everything's fair in fair earnest.

My Deal

OUT OF THE WOODS

In the process of letting go,
you will lose many things from the past,
but you will find yourself.

~DEEPAK CHOPRA

-11-

HEAL-THY CHOICE

A perfect storm

Idiom: The worst possible situation.

I froze. The bull's gaze seemed to be locked on me. Scenes from the bullfight arena came flashing in, as I clutched Amit's hand with my tightest grip.

I looked back to see if we could run. The lane was possibly the narrowest I had ever imagined. At the back, the lane meandered through the old city before vanishing altogether within 100 meters. Right at the swerve, a man in his fifties was squatting on the portico, his face buried in a newspaper. Nonchalant as he was, he barely bothered even to spare a glance at us. The extruding corniche of the immediate mansion (it looked heritage) posed a sprightly invitation, reflecting the morning sun rays right through its fine minarets. Below the architecture, a 20 feet tall gate stood with aplomb atop a couple of stairs. I wished those doors would magically fling open so we could scramble in.

Amit and I were stranded in the middle of the lane, with a massive bull ready to bully at the other end. I dragged my legs slowly, trying not to disturb the quadruped. But they began to hurt again.

'Damn!' I yelled.

I recently had a nagging discomfort in both my legs and was taking pain relievers. It would bring some relief, but only for a short time. In the last couple of months, things had gotten worse, though.

Meanwhile, the bull advanced in its (leisurely) style. Amit looked at me, seeking confirmation for our instincts to react quickly. A bird's-eye view would have undoubtedly made for a classic adventure movie climax, complete with a man versus wild action sequence. A foreign couple also braked pause, bemused at the unfolding of events.

But that action was real.

The bull then abruptly came to a halt. We weren't bullfighters, so we couldn't comprehend such a reflex action. Before Amit and I could turn for a run, we saw a motorcycle emerge from behind the animal. The rider stopped and started feeding it (imagine that for an anti-climax!).

Oh! He's such a saviour!

He could sense our trauma; like a good Samaritan, he smiled and asked, 'First time in Varanasi?'

We nodded like bobbleheads. Amit was like a doubting Thomas, seemingly perturbed by the turn of events.

'Don't worry. These animals are like family to this city. They won't harm'.

We exchanged glances; was it really a storm in a teacup?

December 2019

My visit to Varanasi was in pursuit of solace; a reconciliation with my soul, after my mother passed away that September. It was a life stage transition, and I was fighting hard to overcome a state of depression with her loss.

Mummy had been suffering from arthritis for nearly fifteen years.

It was in December 2019, while in Varanasi, I developed joint pain. My mind was wracked with the dreadful afterthought of inheriting the same. It was an encumbrance brewing. But, in some strange way, I've gained exceptional confidence since then, striving hard to put on a brave face at home and at work. Surprisingly, I was working longer hours and going the additional mile with fresh vigour.

Monday Morning, January 2020

I was all set for the quarterly review. Although the pandemic had not yet manifested itself elsewhere on the planet, its consequences were already being felt. It would be a difficult review. I picked up the laptop and got up for the meeting. I suddenly realised I couldn't walk a foot! Some numbness of sorts had hijacked both my legs, and my knees were hurting like hell. I slumped back on the chair, popped in a tablet, put my head down on my desk and prayed for relief. I cried out in pain.

I've recently had to give up my high-heeled shoes. That was no longer possible due to the persisting agony. I was able to get my hands on some flat bottoms that would release pressure on my ankles quite a bit. But on that day, it seemed insurmountable.

The pain was excruciating. I finished early and went straight home. However, the discomfort persisted. I writhed in agony, and the night was a struggle.

A succession of doctor appointments and therapies followed over the next few weeks.

A full physical examination was overdue. It was a nerve-wracking wait for the findings. It finally surfaced, confirming my worst worries. It was a perfect storm. Every vital parameter appeared to have revolted outside of its bounds.

Arthritis was detected, accompanied by high blood pressure and rising sugar levels. It wasn't simply the ache I was dealing with; my self-esteem had sunk much too quickly. It was a square hole of dread. I had lost both my parents to diabetes, and the fear of inheriting that was unsurmountable. I was engulfed in hopelessness.

I was terrified of going to the doctor. And when I did, it was the least of my expectations that came with it. The doses weighed heavily on my demeanour. These were accompanied by a series of pain relief therapy, physiotherapies, and pain relievers, which were unpleasant and painful.

Flashback

Varanasi

The crimson clouds seemed in a definite rush to embrace the retiring sun. The hue merged with the Ganges beyond the yonder; a canvas smudged with the brush strokes of the master.

I was wandering down the ghat, blissfully unaware of the realities that surrounded me. The twilight was orchestrated to perfection, strumming a soulful elegy.

Mummy, I miss you. Tears kissed my cheeks as I murmured.

Downstream went the boats, almost like silhouettes floating on a mystique river of salvation. The Ganges was calm on the surface. But I could sense the undercurrent inside me. It was a turbulence hard to tame. The smoke had subsided in a far-off pyre, setting free yet another soul in its eternal journey. I couldn't hear a cry. Probably everyone comes to terms as they bid farewell, shedding a tear in silence like me, who lost both her parents in a span of five years.

A sudden breeze played with my shawl, and I struggled to tuck it back. It pushed me to the present. I realised my weary legs couldn't keep up with the beat. I had to pause.

February, 2020

Faridabad

The health report card had shaken me up. So far, none of the treatment was helping the cause. It paled me out gradually.

We eventually found a health counsellor after a frenzied hunt. She helped me see a few simple realities; it all came down to making the right decision.

The Realities

Depression got the better of me which I could not guess by a mile. I was thrown off the driver's seat into a pit of self-pity and inaction. I've been in self-imposed exile since my mother passed away. While Amit, my children, and everyone else were there for me, I huddled into my own world of sadness, remembrance, and seclusion, which was beyond my comprehensible control. It was insidious and kept creeping up over time.

My regular workouts became sporadic, and I stopped going for morning walks. I never realized that my diet was haphazard and that my cortisol levels were dropping drastically. Every single parameter of my physical attributes began to deteriorate, mirroring my deteriorating mental state.

For a health-conscious workaholic like me, it was a harrowing experience with life. As I sank into a ghetto of suppressed emotions, I was caught off guard. The consequences were severe, and they had an unintended impact on my health regimen. It was in the offing, though.

My physician's warnings shook me out of my hazed cocoon. I was standing in front of my bedroom mirror, trying to negotiate with an unfamiliar Deepika. The spirit, the zest, and the vigour all seemed like rusted components in an abandoned garage. The machine itself was bereft of the slightest intent to jump start. I knew I needed to hit the reset button at that very moment.

Fact File

WHO reports that nearly 5% of the world population suffers from depression, out of which the number of women is higher compared to men. Depression took an ugly turn in my case, impacting my health in the worst way possible. It had a cascading effect in pulling me down mentally as well as physically.

During the Speak Up Lady sessions, nearly 70% of the participants confessed they don't have a health regime, be it exercise or health check-ups or adding health supplements to their daily routine.

Nearly 60% said they need permission from their husbands or in-laws to start working out.

Health is where we women tend to compromise, or rather, ignore at will. We will fully spend thousands on our outfits but will run for excuses for a fitter self. When the *Me* in us is ignored, the bigger *We*, our families, are set to face the eventualities.

D's Deal

While a life stage transition affects us mentally, our physical self bears the burnt too. Adjust your clock to fit in a fitness routine before it strikes 12. It pushes your muscles and tissues and powers you back to face, challenge, and overcome any state of limbo you may be in.

My Deal

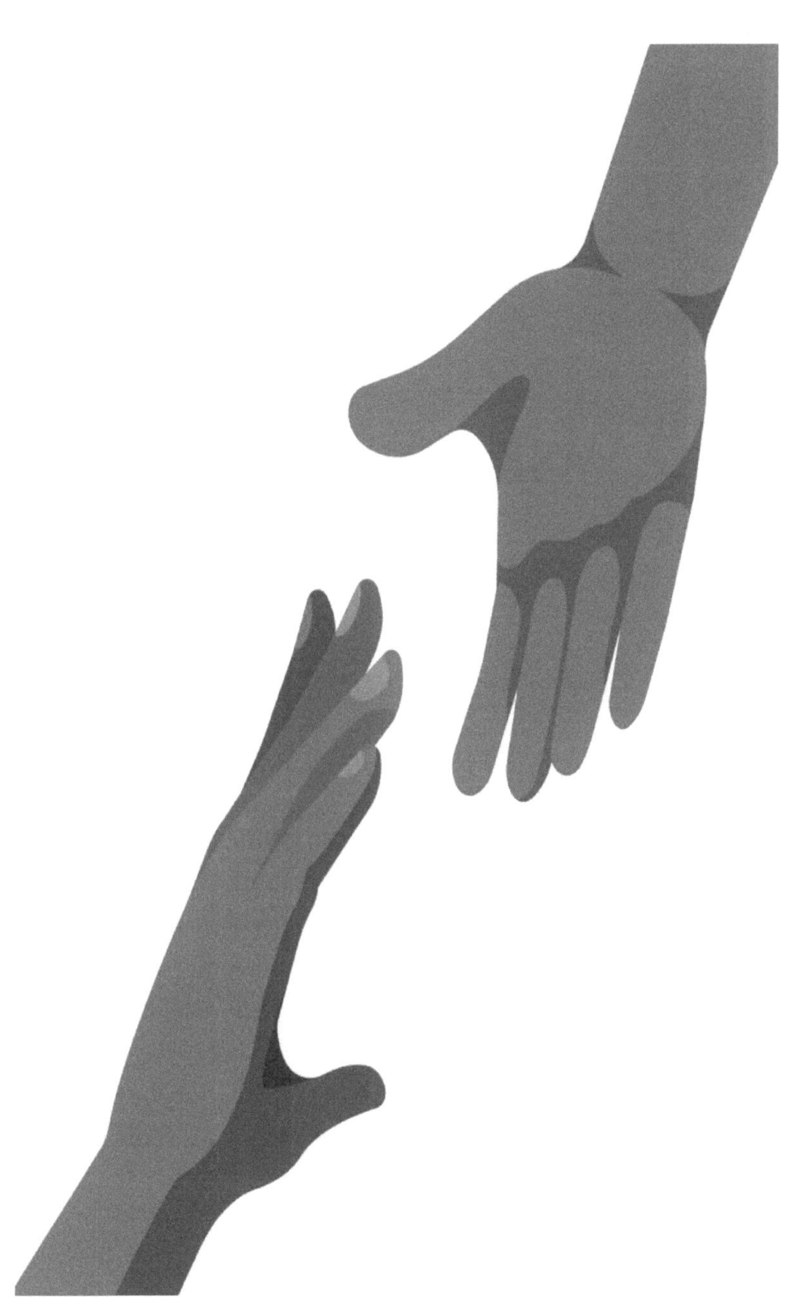

-12-

ASK FOR HELP

In a jam

Noun: In a difficult situation.

I wish I could be in two places at once. This simple, extremely innocent yearning helps to unravel the guilt that resides in me. I wish I could always be into every minute detail while also maintaining my strength, well-being, composure, and creativity. Although such a wish is legitimate, it cannot be fulfilled. I am aware that if I were to attend to every task all day, every day, I would not be the mother and woman I want to be given the family I have, the environment we live in, the job I am in, the work I want to do, and my human wiring. Culturally women in our country are being groomed to own it all, do it all, and all by themselves.

So, knowing what I know, why am I still struggling with this? I recall my mother doing everything on her own.

I would not ask for any help, ideally. Somehow, I have had this belief that asking for help or even letting go would manifest my vulnerability. **I had trained myself to be the superwoman.** Think of it, and I would tune myself to shoulder it all, from preparing food, to driving off in-laws, to taking care of Amit's needs and raising kids. Professionally, I would never sacrifice an agenda. I had grown up cultivating habits that made me feel proud of responsibilities accomplished well.

While I would take up all the responsibility, plan and strive towards completing every task, but would feel guilty of procrastinating or unaccomplishments, if any. Interestingly, when you can't manage everything, it's okay to let go. But the idea itself sounds regressive, isn't it? That's how I had trained myself to think and believe all these years.

Research found that 96% of women experience guilt at least once per day. This may even contribute to the beginning of depression and have detrimental effects on our health.

Things didn't affect me much earlier. But, as I added numbers to my age, I was losing out on so many things I always ignored.

I wasn't as energetic. *Take it or lose it, Deepika,* my mind would remind me. I got stuck in my role at the office. I wanted to but lacked the confidence to ask for bigger and more challenging projects. I was chasing time, leaving my own self behind. **On the contrary, I had just one thing to do; ask for help.**

It's a widespread misperception that asking for assistance denotes weakness. When we ask for help, we frequently feel like we're imposing or inadequate. This is not at all the case. Asking for assistance when you need it demonstrates strength and confidence, so you shouldn't feel bad about it. Well, I didn't realize it until I met Roopa.

Superwoman

It was around early 2000.

I wanted to earnestly take up the upcoming transition project at the office. I had been waiting for this opportunity for quite some time now. It was a global initiative and promised an enormous opportunity to collaborate with counterparts across Europe. However, my existing profile back then had been miser in allowing a breather (or, maybe, the superwoman in me made me rigid). Every task was nothing less than a priority. Moreover, the upcoming exam schedule of my kids had flagged a red alert in the interim. My March calendar was full.

I shut my laptop and packed up for the day.

'I do not understand how you guys work nowadays', my father-in-law would comment. 'I know Papa', I would jokingly interrupt him, 'it wasn't the case during your times'. Papa would stare point-blank and say nothing. It would make me more uncomfortable.

Suddenly, the lifestyle became increasingly demanding; in-laws with failing health requiring frequent medical attention, kids' studies pruning their freeways, stretched working hours with limited physical movement, all of it.

The Memorable Monday

That Monday was scheduled to be another marathon to kick start the week. A couple of senior leadership meetings were on the agenda. The second half, however, held an exciting promise; a mentoring session with Roopa, one of our senior directors.

Plutarch once said that 'our mind is not a vessel that needs filling, but woods that need igniting.'

I had no clue how that would translate into action, but I was looking forward to that session. I knew I needed answers to get unstuck and hoped the session might help.

We were 10 women colleagues, with Roopa as the senior executive mentor helming the show.

Orange was the colour of the day, at least so it seemed. Roopa was clad in a vibrant orange saree, oozing confidence and candour. She had an infectious aura which could transcend the physical distance, underlining the mark of a virtuoso in business.

Roopa was a natural storyteller. She took us through her breath-taking career progression in an entertaining 15-minute narration. I was on a roller-coaster as she navigated through the ebbs and flows. It was a rollicking story of a rockstar in action.

As soon as she finished, I raised my hand.

'Roopa, there are so many glass ceilings in the working world for women, still you have grown so rapidly…what's your secret sauce?'

Roopa smiled, 'Asking for what you want, asking for support whenever needed, asking for the project you want to undertake… **ASK! It's possibly one of the shortest three-letter words but holds immense potential to fetch you whatever you desire or intend!** Glass ceilings will continue to exist…At least don't create your own glass ceiling or if you have created one, then break it!'

Richard Dawkins famously quoted, 'The solution often turns out more beautiful than the puzzle.' For me, the solution lay in that three-letter word; ASK.

The Transition Project

Things wouldn't change in a day, but I had to sustain the inertia. The transition project was inviting a call to action. But I couldn't gather strength until I met Roopa.

A simple word has the potential to untangle a complicated equation. It's the power of expression that such words entail. But it's pivotal to imbibe the essence in its entirety before applying it.

Roopa's suggestions reverberated in my head. Believing in something is easier than putting it into action. You need to bridge the chasm to walk over to confidence. Yet, I had to try.

Is it that simple? I asked myself. I had never done this before.

Here's the point; as women, what do we convince ourselves about? Is it fear of failure, the guilt of vulnerability, or simply our inability to let go?

I decided to go for the Transition Project. But a puzzle had to be solved. Layers of beliefs took to be dusted. I had a hard look at my official calendar and home tasks. I would need to make many adjustments; manage tasks, ask for help, delegate a few to Amit at home, and ask for help from my team. I knew I had to tell my boss that I was ready for the project.

Maybe it's too much at stake just for a project, I thought.

Amit sensed my dilemma.

'Do you need any help?' Amit asked me at the dinner table.

I was taken aback by the point-blank question. *How the hell did he guess?* I thought. I told him about the project but was quick to list down the deliverables and tasks at hand. 'I'm concerned, Amit. I don't think I can do justice to the project with so much at stake'.

Amit smiled. 'You don't have to do everything, do you? Didn't we manage it before? Every little thing doesn't need to be perfect. If you want to be part of the project, so be it. What makes you think you will be offered a chance without even asking for it? Go, raise your hand'.

It was such a reassurance, first from Roopa and then Amit.

After dinner, I picked up my laptop for one last time that evening. I started typing my email…

Dear Shallabh,

Hope you are doing well. I wanted to reach out to you to share that I want to raise my hand to do the Portugal transitions.

I have 15 years of experience and have handled 5 major global transition projects. If it's convenient, I wish to block 20 mins with you to talk about this further.

Thank you for all your guidance & support

Best regards

D's Deal

Raise your hand and ask for help without any qualms. The world will respond.

My Deal

-13-

WORK BACK HOME

In a word of one syllable

Idiom: Explicit, coherent, logical.

When My Children Were Young

It takes a lot of guts to be a working mother, that too putting up with in-laws and managing the house order.

Does that sound cliche? It sounds so for some, but I have seen women buckling under pressure. Resultant: quitting the job they otherwise loved the most. Furthermore, a sense of guilt stays on forever: either you stay put or quit for good.

Is there a midway? Neo-liberals will be at loggerheads on this.

When I see working mothers face these deafening challenges till date, I pause. Questions pop up left, right, and centre…

- What does it take to be uncompromising yet balanced?
- What must one do to not feel hapless?

Work-life balance as a concept is dated now. While we as women always assume we are perfect in balancing out things, in essence, we are **Shakti.** We are **Oorja.** We are energy, which is not just balanced, but a concoction of integration; integration of clarity, understanding, vision, and empathy. That's who we are. Hence, work-life integration is the norm.

That undeniably calls for enhanced responsibility, not just leadership. So, what does work-life integration mean? How do we chart it out? Where does it begin, and how does it expand?

Clarity Begins with Self

On my return to India, I took up a job at Times Bank. My kids were small, my son was in KG, and my daughter was still to step into the premises. My in-laws always wished their daughter-in-law to be a teacher (which I was not), who could spend quality time with the kids. I am a workaholic and love my job equally the way I love my family. And that was the sole reason I had to find the elusive mid-way. I had no choice but to find a solution, which at that point in time, I thought was work-life balance. Such was the jargon which we would refer to.

Much later, as my kids grew and I grew alongside them, I did realize it was more of integration of efforts that helped me sustain balance for so long.

Little Kids Went for Tuition

As they were growing up, I decided to send them for tuition once they were back from school. It was a bold decision, much against my in-laws' will. There were struggles, misunderstandings, and heartburns (possibly).

It's a common saying, *nalayak bachhe* tuition *letey hai* (dumb students go for tuition). Is it truly so? My in-laws also had concerns about wasting money on tuition, and that my kids would become dependent on tutors. I had to explain that when I would return home, I would not spend time getting their home tasks completed. That would invariably make me scold them when they would make any mistake. I would not tread that path. I would rather spend quality time with my kids, preparing them for competitions, rehearsing dramas, and reading stories. I wanted to create good memories with them.

Once my son would come back from school, he would freshen up, have his lunch, and head towards his tuition class with our neighbour, who stayed right opposite. At times, he would take his siesta at her place. He would complete his homework and studies under her supervision.

Once I was back home, it was the creative sessions that we three would engage in. But why creative?

I would rather engage my kids in activities which were beyond the regular haggle. Kids need more proactive home schooling than being trapped within the confines of templated education.

My ultimate objective was to put things into a structure which would be smooth. If I had to spend twelve hours at the office, then my time must be spent productively and joyously with my family and kids.

What it did to my kids was that they became independent. Drishti still teases me by asking what made me so structured. I had to, because that let me do things I wanted to and included my family as well to be a part of that auto-pilot mode.

Management lessons I learnt at work like governance, coordination, and skills, I applied at home. Even though I didn't sit down with them with their home tasks, I was updated on every aspect of their progress, I was in constant touch with the teachers, and I never missed any PTA.

And whatever human values I learnt at home; I took those to my workplace.

Don't you resonate with the fact that the lockdown has taught us integration and balance? I believe it has.

I changed jobs but made sure I opted for a branch closer to my home so that I would not miss my children whenever I wanted to see them.

For me, working has been a priority because that's my identity. I could not let that slip away. Instead of cribbing about my job, which was never easy any which way, I would rather talk about the better things that happened at work at the dinner table. That ensured two things, one, I was not disrespecting my job, which I was proud of, and two, my family also realized the responsibilities I had as a senior leader in the organization. I valued myself, and so did my ecosystem.

D's Deal

Bring your value to the table, be it at work or at home. Else no one will understand your stance; leave aside appreciating it. The onus lies on us and how we plan our life. Either we juggle to balance or be smart to integrate.

My Deal

NEW WAY
OLD WAY

-14-

WHEN YOU LET GO

Heebie-jeebies

Idiom: A state of nervousness, fear, or anxiety.

It Was My Fault

Even when my son was 2 years old, he wouldn't speak. He would ask for everything through gestures; whether he was thirsty or hungry, whether he wanted to go out to play, or reach out for his toys.

My entire family was scared, fearing the worst… would he never speak?

We took him to speech therapists, the best of them. But it didn't work. We explored all possible medical solutions and suggestions.

I had almost given up. I remember taking him to AIIMS for a hearing test. Abhinav cried so much. But no medical issue was identified.

We couldn't hold him back for long indoors. Finally, we sent him to the play school. Within a couple of days, my son started speaking. That may sound too miraculous, but that's precisely what happened. And honestly, we were clueless.

I went back to the doctor to seek an explanation as to what really happened and how he could start speaking while every treatment failed.

The doctor said, I remember it distinctly, 'You didn't let him grow. You got him everything he wanted right up to him without him asking for it even.'.

That seemed to be a statement too psychological from a paediatrician. I wasn't convinced. Now I realize what made me rigid to that statement of the doctor. I, as a mother, never gave in to the fact that it was my fault in taking care of my own child. Just as an unrelenting, possessive mother would react, and so did I.

2020, The Story Repeats

I remember discussing the impossible during coffee breaks during the day at the office. 'Imagine how life would be if we could hop out of the office and hop into the bedroom!'

We used to make fun of each other's wild imaginations. But the unimaginable happened. The pandemic struck.

The WFH was cool (in casuals and Tees), but when you are all by yourself at your makeshift desk, and the roads are empty as drought, time flies without announcing the end of the day. The silence grew on us, and that unmasked a rarity; the lost birdsong filled the city. Peacocks were spotted dancing at the traffic signals, and some rare species had a gala time without provocation. The world returned to its natural best, while we were adapting to a new way of life.

Mornings meandered into evenings, yet I seemed to be in a time warp. Till the time Mary would knock on the door and remind me, 'It's 9 p.m. Didi', I would remain locked over VCs. This became a routine, and now I wonder how we adapted to this lifestyle with ease (?). The house turned into a world of cubicles for Amit and me.

Soon, my kids, Abhinav, and Drishti would join us back home. College and Office got into the WFH mode as the pandemic had its say in every little thing we created as a human society.

Drishti had called over one of her closest friends to stay with us as she couldn't make her way back to her hometown with the sudden developments.

She was known to us for a long time, and oftentimes she stayed up at our place. It was more of welcoming them back.

I was happy for both my kids. It was family time again after a long gap. The mother in me was even more excited.

The initial euphoria was unabated. I would invest more time in the kitchen to prepare the best dishes inspite a full day at work. There was spring in my feet. After such a long gap, it felt like home again! Breakfast, lunch, and dinner would be laid out as per the old timetable. And I would announce, *Breakfast is ready!*

None of the kids would answer. I would call up twice, thrice, and... still, there wouldn't be any reply. Amit would remind me, 'they have been working up all night... let them take their time'. But I would argue.

'Why so? This has never been their routine, Amit! It's family time. They must join'.

However, all my arguments would meet a No-Reply. They would drag themselves out half asleep on the table with no conversations happening. The purpose was not food but togetherness and family conversations.

Kids would wake up late into the day. By then, it would be lunchtime. Invariably, all my hard work on the elaborate breakfast menu would go to waste. It was becoming increasingly agitating for me. Suddenly, I could sense a loss of control over the proceedings in home affairs. I was angry and confused at the same time.

One evening, I vented out my frustrations on Drishti. I was well prepared to face all the counter arguments. I went on for ten odd minutes. Drishti listened silently. Finally, she broke her silence.

'Mummy, bhai has joined us after six years. I have been away for the last three years. Our lives have changed since we left.

Our work schedules are different. We lead a different routine. You need to realize that. Why don't you let go and accept these facts?'

Drishti continued, 'let's all give ourselves a little space and learn new ways of living together to include all working hours and schedules.'

I was stunned and silenced.

D's Deal

The same resounds at your workplace too. As a leader, learn the art of letting go. Governance is essential, but overdoing it leads to stifling the team. You need to understand the thin line and respect it as a leader. Do not hold on to everything which may be impossible for you to pursue with the same earnestness throughout. Once you let go, you allow yourself to grow by focusing on other strategic aspects, and by doing so, you let your team grow with freedom of thought and responsible actions. Learning new ways of working and flexi hours, including all work styles, why is it so difficult for us to imbibe?

My Deal

D’s Deals

IT'S TIME YOU SPEAK UP!

For each one of us, our life lessons are markers of change; change of perspectives, realizations, and applications. But the extent we emphasize on the applications makes a world of difference. Is it restricted to our own selves, or do we go beyond and spread the word? Are we still in the garb of I, me and myself or do we feel the urge to evolve and check on the problems of a cohort in the society we live in? Problems do exist, but not every bit of it is manifested for obvious reasons and beyond. So, whatever we learn, we must plan to put up a success story and then, if you hear me, help create multiple such stories of triumph with people around.

Rediscover Yourself

Challenge your own self, if need be, to discover the real you. That doesn't mean you necessarily sacrifice your aspiration but ask yourself whether you would sprint up the tarmac of success or should you analyse the repercussions in advance; interpersonal, social, or professional. We tend to get blinded by the strobe lights of awesomeness. But I insist you pause. You may argue, what if I lose a golden opportunity if I let go of this? True, it's unnerving. Take a pause, think, consult, absorb, and then make your decision. If you are concerned about building your own brand, then it's just not you who makes it… it's the whole gang of followers who cheerlead you in your journey. So, it will be your final take to take it or let go.

Me vs. We

We talk about serving the larger WE, as in our community. But the moment the ME, as in our own self, is challenged, we recoil into our survival instincts. Only if we bring out the gritty Tasneem in us we can possibly rewrite a script that can change pre-sets and mindsets.

Un-Colour Your Beliefs

Colours don't define characters. Belief does.

In an ironic twist, in a culture enamoured with white skin, vitiligo is regarded as unclean, unsightly, and more of a nuisance than an ailment. Super models like Chantelle Brown-Young do lift our spirits, but only just like a plus-sized model would.

During my Speak Up Lady sessions, I have had participants with dark skins who were tormented beyond bet to even switch on their videos. Such has been their trauma. With Divya and Rashmi as my role models, I believe we do have a conversation starter.

Taxonomy Matters

Mind your language because changing overviews of gen-next can become overwhelming. Are we not biased by our innate beliefs of stereotypes and orthodoxy? Don't you think life has many more surprises than we expect? How do we react when such disruptions shake us up? Better be prepared, being flexible enough to adjust to the paradigm shifts. Else, be prepared for challenges you may never overcome.

What we believe in as parapets, may not be valid from a broader perspective. It may not even stand a chance in future conversations and evolving societal matrices. What may sound simple, obvious, and rational, may need a deeper introspection of root cause analysis, provided we can challenge ourselves to it. The question remains, will you let that be?

As women we are groomed to be conservative with our perception, which may be limited by knowledge and experience. However, time reveals the truth. At times, it hits hard, and later, it heals. It's valid in both the personal and professional spaces we operate. It's prudent not to jump to conclusions fast. You never know, events may surprise you.

Go for Grit

It is about challenging yourself, not protocols. That would be a crime. But when your desire for something great overpowers you, go for it. Remember, everything's fair in fair earnest.

While a life stage transition affects us mentally, our physical self bears the brunt too. Adjust your clock to fit in a fitness routine fast. It pushes your muscles and tissues and powers you back to face, challenge, and overcome any state of limbo you may be in.

Raise your hand and ask for help without any qualms. The world will respond.

Bring your value to the table, be it at work or at home. Else no one will understand your stance, leave aside appreciating it. The onus lies on us, and how we plan our life. Either we juggle to balance or be smart to integrate.

As a leader, learn the art of letting go. Governance is essential, but overdoing it leads to stifling the team. You need to understand the thin line and respect it as a leader. Do not hold on to everything which may be impossible for you to pursue with the same earnestness throughout. Once you let go, you allow yourself to grow by focusing on other strategic aspects, and by doing so, you let your team grow with freedom of thought and responsible actions. Learning new ways of working and flexi hours, including all work styles, why is it so difficult for us to imbibe?

Contact: deepika@deepikachawla.com

9 789355 544445

Printed by Libri Plureos GmbH in Hamburg,
Germany